Cry of the No-No

Cry of the No-No

Sebastian Schloessingk

GOMETRA

© Sebastian Schloessingk 2017
Cover Painting © Alba Lydia
Schloessingk 2017
Frontispiece by Robert
Gibbings © NCB 1939
Printed and bound
in Great Britain
by IngramSpark
Set in Adobe
Garamond Pro on
14th September 2017
by Roc Sandford at
the Gometra Press
a sister imprint of Soho

ISBN 978-1-900389-02-0

For Melanie

Table of Contents

An Entire Word 1
Infallible Targets 2
Left Lane 3
International Call, and How's 4
Coddled 5
Each to His 6
Free Ride 7
Giant Thing 8
Road Safety 9
Breast Horses, 2011 10
Shepherd Soft-shod 12
The Mix 14
Spill 15
In Column Days 16
At the Last, in Her Bothy 17
Rec.Mem.Game 18
Thins 20
The Draw 22
Perk 23
Hoots 25
Sofa Cigarette Hole 27
Claimant 29
Condamn'd 30
Traversal 31
Timeless Fernlike Party Horns 32
Deal with It 33
The Tuft, the Pierced Throne and the English Duke 35
Sacred Shell 36
Facebook 37
Shove Ten 38
The Residue 39
County Town Pre-Christmas 40

Bump and Slash   41
Cameraderie   42
We All Call Her That   43
Shotput   45
Leaf Couplet   46
Done Good   47
The Taxi Stand, South Wales   48
Guest on Guest   49
Train of Empties   50
The Cladding   51
Denounce   52
Core Clubs   53
Teamwork   54
Wales   55
The Grater   56
A Size or More Down   57
A Sprinkling   58
Warszawa-Paris   60
From the Stack, at a Slant   61
Separate Sightings   62
Planted in the Back of Our Minds   63
Handover by Night   64
Attached Cabin   65
Cloud Measure   67
Woven Alike   68
Surrender Hanky   69
In the Lieu   70
Thought Through   72
Ledges   73
Whichever   74
Tourists at the End   75

An Entire Word

He confided to me over the washing-up,
youngish tousled and Irish-jawed, the other day
he'd heard someone say 'ointment'. It came to him
that he never said 'ointment' himself, never had
said it, there was a gap, extending back.
He excused the triviality. I said not
at all, I knew what he meant, the shock of the sad
dormant small-deal absence. A measureless omission
at the chemist's, and an exile from the soothing
application at home, from the tube, of the word.
The whole world of ointment-saying missed out on.

Infallible Targets

It's on the (minor) way back
of hand, from putting onto shelf,
into fridge, that other things like bowls
of sentimental value and
shapely target jugs get brushed,
teeter and fall four feet for
a long time because it is their fate
and smash despite the last-second
manoeuvrings of our feet because
we are not the prehensiles we were.

It is on the minor way
back down mountain, in the failing
light after a great success
against the summit's champagne
sky, on the long col between
achieving and rest, in the gullies
of infrangible rock strung with
snow at its most dark-apparent,
that we slip hurtle and die.
Happened on the minor way back.

Left Lane

The contrails in late blue, their abridged strokes –
those inching on out, those from nowhere inserted –
were aligned, wherever, like single-minded
eels homing up a river. Night fell: a rabbit
after healthy zig-zagging in the headlights thought best
to sprint back under the tyres. Delicate, definite
sound – not troubling hard tyres but the soft brain
(in charge of a machine in charge of another).

Dawn broke cloudy, damp colourful trees, grey fugitive
ostrich farm ostrich on the road, pacing ahead
in the correct lane but viewed from a car behind
some uncertainty in the body language.

International Call, and How's

She had a cold, he replied, and was snoring.
I said, 'Strange, when the weaker sex snores.'
Sort of threatening. Yes, to take over the world,
he felt. World domination threat, I agreed.

Coddled

Sleep is very much what you want when you're happy
and when you're unhappy. It's the one event
totally as good as anticipated, every
time (at long last in the dark, almost im-
plausibly, I climb in). Sometimes on waking
I notwithstanding need to put crude daylight

between me and a nightmare. Conversely, dreamt
recently of these words to be skewered, coddled
and brought to the day, by repeating: *Skydive
From The Pulpit*. Excuse me? *Under*slept, now,
(dignity the slowest restored) means a stream
of my jokes, so-so till dusk. But when it's all cloudy

on holiday in the car, same tendency – attracting
same slagging off, from her. Still, as they sleep
a woman holds a man, overheating and causing
him to have a bad dream of their separation.
Which vanishes as soon as she rolls away and
they are together again, thank you very much.

Each to His

Indoors on the ferry – all untowardly
enveloped, the sitting with a sickly inert
bias, but screens and chips, the smell of chips
innate here – the stout boy walked with his mother,
examined the pale grey sea in the window's
condensation and said 'I should think there's quite
a few sharks and the odd whale' (in it). Perfect
strange normal *Creature Comforts* locution.
On the ferry deck nearer dusk, facing full-scale
louringness, red sun funnelled through low slats – mean wind
having seen off everyone else – an albino
ranged, with shoulder-white hair, the rose sleight of eye,

a sharp curving nose and a carrier bag. In three
-quarter-length trousers, young solitary and
not scarless, peering seaward or upward. Chiefly at
two big seabirds, gannets with yolk tint and rapacious
mascara, sliding about not far above him.
From his carrier bag he fetched a short specialist
telescope, two-joint spyglass type, applied it
to his rare British eye, and looked up locked on.
A seabird himself by feature, in a dangled
camouflage jacket and slamming wind, he rated
every bit as mystical as the boy indoors.

Free Ride

I first tried that side-squinch of the mouth –
to lay out distaste or disappointment –
in pure imitation of what Obama
and the young gymnast alongside, female
Olympic medallist (*but* the silver),
did in unison at a White House photo opp.
A year later and I've learnt it maybe too well,
pull it at all kinds of odd moments mostly
in private, not so much expressing
such feelings as promptly letting such feelings,
not particularly in evidence beforehand,
clamber opportunistically aboard the squinch.

Giant Thing

God parted his fingers upon
the (flat screen of the) Earth
and drew up mountains,
for scrutiny.
But it was from down in the caves
that Christ The Speleologist
was borne out at last
into the air. Having suffered

a rockfall onto the head
2 km into the network
Riesending. And been rescued
by seven hundred in chains
or teams over eleven days.

Wrapped and bearded on his stretcher
and motionless and face up
he came out. Lifted from the deep
Cross of Tunnel and Cave
by a throng (with sky behind)
in his upward absorptive eyes.

Road Safety

Of course, she said, nobody hitches
any more: either the driver or
the hitcher is a serial killer,
no use pretending otherwise.
So it *is* safe, I probed, if you're
a serial killer yourself, chances
that *both* of you are serial killers
have got to be low. And anyway
if you both are, you can always
get your mojo working first.

Breast Horses, 2011

There are floods everywhere without comment.
And afterstatement nods (that came from China) – those
burgeoning afternods on the news, to (woodpecker-)frank
the point the self waylaid on high street has made.
There's 'upspeak' everywhere so as *not* to make the point
too much: narrations and facts rising tentative
(out of fearless Australia, this), very inclusive. And
loads of 'likes', like a bunch of them in each sentence

(50s and 60s in source, bottled in California,
re-released). It's all good globalization, but
without any comment as to the churning brown floods
(always breaking the banks of living memory)
being part of Climate Change or not. There are large
families in any country but only for the richest
and the poorest. And beauty contests for breast horses,
amplified pouts, with judges that are connoisseurs

gauging every implant, nose tweak, buttock rebuilt.
But Class War, forget it. Intelligence War
has writhed into view: the patently subtle
of whatever hue a gross insult, to all creationist
white 'open carry' folk. There are social networks
like dropped heaps of Mikado needles. Then the new
individual human right enshrined, to a just as
valid opinion, inviolate: any ('that's *your* …')

answering logic is barefaced diss. And the tasty
growing flaw (among two or three) in democracy: counters

don't count, announcers announce, denouncers are denounced.
There is the relief of falling among muslims
on the Harrow Road in a Lebanese café,
Al-Jazeera up on the screen, not greatly watched,
and everyone at separate tables so quiet
and sane, a downbeat oasis not downcast.

Shepherd Soft-shod

For children swings and roundabouts,
and on through life it's swings and
roundabouts, but for old people

crowns and bridges (see also
'of thorns' and 'of sighs'). When you
have little, you like songs of loss

and songs of plenty, when you have
plenty you like songs of plenty
but not songs of loss.

Everyone's task being simple:
to give a good story to the
character with a name

(theirs) and shepherd the story
to closure. Having begun to
feel (first shafts of relief)

that from here with a stretched few
bounding steps, soft-shod feet
turned out, you could make nothing less

than the tightrope's far end, high small
square platform and professional
perch of death. With life conveyed past all

the terrors, pole antennae wide.
Though equally you imagine
someone's brusque step off

at suicide not because
of disaster befallen but
because none has befallen yet

and they want to keep it that way.
In either case next: wild, banal
swings and pulsings of the rope.

The Mix

On New Year's morning 'sweating out the toxins'
(her words) in my arms. My coming to bed
mostly much later and 'sucking up the warmth

with your ice-cold bum'. Hot water bottle
advice osmosis. Told her I added always
some prudent cold water, she said no need.

Reminded me, a year on, be sure to mix
the cold in. What? Oh that, long since
ditched, no need I blandly reply.

On planes the seat swap treaty (she's tried
window seats, but claustrophobia;
the aisle brings on my people issues). And

with 'Your third eye's flaky' she offended me.
Her own Langlauf on Elliptical Strider
just as scary, revealed by the opening door

gradually. I prefer this exercise, him-
and-her-lying-alongside *perpetuum
mobile:* she in her nightie up-hoiks

both legs (for stomach muscles), up goes his head
(for stomach muscles and a closer look).
Down go her legs, back sinks his head. And repeat.

Spill

The Farm Supplies shop owner, short and hale
and dignified, whose business runs
lower and lower, whose white beard remains
nice trimmed, and whose sports jacket is still
the voice of The Country, his silence burst
in upon for a humble bag of birdseed,
spilt the entire sack in a corner of the dingy
neat cluttered shop-hut and heaved an *'Oh Shavings!'*.

The cry resounded quite insufficient
for this cruel event. Shavings is what
hamsters neglected in their cage sometimes eat.
It constipates them, ejects their wronged
pink stomach behind like a slow-down parachute
and does for them. So the cry did sort
of express it, the dry-eyed shop owner's
small-world noble and constipated despair?

In Column Days

It has been known for a Lonely Hearter
to yes be lassoed with felt-tip by another
and rung. She was out. He left a message.
She waited weeks. Then rang back, left a message.
The try fizzled out with cold feet, they never
met by arrangement. But a while later

out of all the Guardian Lonelies of
London they met by chance, and married.
The joy of company and the rigour
of self-restraint, that's marriage. Now Fred
Astaire and Ginger Rogers did arrange
to meet continually, for successive

films of dance and romance. But their mouths
never met, didn't visibly kiss, the camera
by then had glided in an arc behind one
of the amorous heads, or the next scene
had slipped its arm around the film's waist.
Some waists, it is known, during not so much

film-making as love-making, slosh about under.
When a girl, a woman, has drunk to excess,
a combination of the sheer swilling
amount and the stomach muscles' own
wine-dunked flaccidity may have that
effect. The Heart Is A Lonely Punter.

At the Last, in Her Bothy

When my aunt received me with closed eyes it was clear
she didn't know who she was receiving but she knew
where she sought admittance. Her lids, shut but not
screwed tight, seemed to state in their proper convexity
that we shouldn't really have emerged at all, light (same as
fire) was a mistake. Cheek to pillow, her face collapsed
sideways by gravity, the lids linked by a profound
age gash across the bridge of the nose. Her upper cheek
– both of them concave at the best of times – now fell away
into a trench that became her mouth, itself displaced
down (toward the regions where she wanted to go).
And at intervals throughout the visit groaning in a
low-pitched unselfconscious voice. Once or twice when I'd laid
palm on her forehead or knuckle, she opened her eyes, lucid
briefly, saw me, and was appalled by the inference
she was still alive. She reclosed her lids, around the two fresh
impalements of world-distress, and out of her came *'Oh please ...'*

Rec.Mem.Game

Believe in the Battersea Rotor?
Remember and almost believe, my turn.
The two-way wrist-burn? Definitely, in
focus like a watchface, it's weird,

tormented incredulous skin getting hotter
but ugly setback explained. *Chinese Burn.*
(Indian Burn.) Whereupon you grin.
Next up ... the goldfish scatter-feed?

Goldfish. I thumbnail open
the mini cardboard cylinder's disc-top,
strew in the bowl the pungent dismal-futile
flakes, they don't sink, go on smelling on the water

and the fish it could be I don't love go on
dying. In fairground clear bags hung, swam, plopped ...
Battersea Funfair through trees though, I'll
never see again except for The Rotor.

Lined up in a circle – suspects
gormlessly varied in height, or folk dance pod
shoved out facing leery. The grubby red rubbery
sides began to spin, mechanically the floor

was taken from us, some caught in aspic,
others slithered some and their skirts rode
up despite their hands – the Marilyn club.
You're a boy and crane against the G-force

manfully at high speed just to half-sit but if
you're a teddy-boy you stood right out like your own quiff.
Rim and the winklepickers belting round creepy,
quiff to the dead-slow-turn centre of the EP.

Thins

Gimme Shelter, the US tour, and the one
free open-air concert. Caused a youth migration
as of bison (in VW vans) that could be tracked
from above, converging for hundreds of miles.
Like a ripple reversed, to where The Stones chose
to drop in. Some of the young male bison climbed,
as the hour approached, the sound and lighting scaffolds

around the stage in broad day. Thin and long-haired
as anyone, and British with an early
drooping classless accent modelled on Jagger's,
the stage manager took the mike, pleaded:
'Can we have some REASON! – *whatever that is.*'
The subversive end clause tacked on late
in a bankrupt flurry, when he realized

the word he'd used, even stressed. What a square,
what a clerk, what a drag. He stands corrected
(in T-shirt) for all time not only by the agile
scaffold pioneers (no sillier than
Harrison Ford in Witness). But the flapping penis
on a bearded youth-hippy, tanned, short, slight,
vital rather than strong, dancing trance-naked

alone in a tiny tolerant clearing of crowd
– sun as bidden, grass ground warmth – at another
rock festival (spread out into lore). His long dark hair
matched by a black lower mop, a splurge, with

the pallid modest penis glimpsably flapping
somewhere in it. Not swayed by reason or thinking
twice about the minutiae of his carnal shell.

The Draw

A competition to find the world's
most evocative sound has been won
by the seagull's cry. Raw tones
layering up, each seagull outcry plied
(before it's through) with another and

another, converging in the grey
above the stern. Or fleeting, no
mistaking, over an urban roof, who
knows why but with the big sea tang.
Distance-going, notched into paintings

(for look and for sound) by maître
as by child: those two-curve shorthand
cleavage squiggles above the slacker
curves of the sea. In Cardiff Bay –
its malleable boardwalk and Café Rouge –

the winning entry can also be heard.
Out over the water but not far,
from a speaker limpeted half way
up a pole. In lieu of, or to draw
gulls and people Cardiff Bay.

Perk

Who cares about thinning that's (tackily) greying?
It's doing me a **?*ing service,
a savage trim would do me a greater

and the New Universal Remedy
shaven dome with telltale blue zones
and fellow-traveller-assisted kudos

the greatest I reckon but girlfriend's stark no.
What can you say? The daylight in dark
city plate glass seizes the grey till it shouts.

And then (dining out) the low-slung bulb's
chic light battens on your pretty sad patch.
What's the evolutionary basis

of balding, the perk? – mused a buddy (under
smug full canopy). Obvious, I grudged,
attacks the disease of perfectionism

two ways. *Narcissus* meets his biggest
slap in the head, and *Hislop* establishes,
weekly, that his sixty tenacious tophairs

are priceless and see-through fringelet all right
(stop counting from max, get a load of
parliaments across the globe, from the rear).

All the same the mortification
when, peering into swimwater,
your child disconcerted puts in 'Dad,

I can see a bit of skin.' And, deep down
with prehuman expressionless hair
circumwafting, you mutter where.

Child innocence, rooted in the height gap.
How about a comb-over whirlpool
confected so high only God gets a glimpse in?

What do ageing men have six of, others five,
(9,8,6)? Hint: forehead, most of penis,
palms, nails, soles ... Perfectly Hairless Places.

Hoots

Reversing (via the mirror)
stonily face forward
between hedges with reluctance is
today the rural male norm.
Men rubbernecking, so passé.

A 4×4 three cars ahead
cooled itself, the elephant spray
trumpeted high above windscreen
dappling the car behind, which
hosed off in turn and dappled the next.

There's an epidemic in Britain
of hooting, on the part of the overtaken.
Out of nothing, protesting at the
mere fact, and flashing with diseased
character from the straight road behind.

Somehow this sits with the headlong patience,
the transcendent willingness to crawl
complete miles to a roundabout, round it
crawl, and plump for the one clogged-off
exit: *more* jam, to the horizon.

But free – the pissing Scotsmen
in a service station toilet. Carroty
wigs, kilts flicked up onto shoulders,
football questions chipped in by
leftmost urinal chieftain …

Airport carparks seen from the sky
used to sing out the British choice of red
(recurring, to yield a delayed
Daltonist test dot letter). Now silver-grey
the nation opting looms, round every ...

Sofa Cigarette Hole

Ageing hydraulically, with steam hisses
as we stoop down. Granny, when she turned
the TV off, put a dipping emphasis
on the remote, a flourish to make sure, and

turned to speak but couldn't, loud telly
had *come back on* (her grip still flourished
the sleek control). This happened every time.
And to a Sikh (at the doctors' group practice)

with diffident son walking before: forlorn
deep-bent knees were happening, the trembling
convulsive inch-stamping of his way forward
like a Flamenco performer. The legs'll

go first, say football pundits. Tell me
about it, leaden sprint, arms a blur. Twenty
paces slower and one optometrist line
wavering shrunk (binned). Towards our worn

sofa Granny, on her repeat
visits, plunged back at 32 ft per
sec^2. She had to let stiff shanks
lost bony in limp black trousers travel

on, onward … bounce off low springs a bit.
And the Halloween pumpkin's teeth
– orange, triangular – are caving in,
mumbling in with time. Will we all meet

as given in Heaven? Or will it be
the heaven of old age – jealousy
dead, old flames come in from the cold,
stand round, or will Viagra fuck with that?

Claimant

The Belgian wood, where two paths sombre down
to merge under heavier-grouped boughs –
a stone embedded, close to a trunk.
Resolute compact tablet; yellow
flowers jut bundled from a pot at its base
as if from the inky forest floor off-season.
The flowers – at first screened by the blond
strict hair of a friend (wan down her coat) wending
introductorily ahead, soundless –
come as the jolt. And dispose you to receive
the words from the dimmered milieu of wood
a squat tablet wanted. In suffered gold letters
and two careful languages instructing
the 'wanderer' to think of a dead man entitled
Ruyskenvelde. 1957. The two
wanderers have to exchange as signs
of living unspoken a stunted question:
How would you like a grave, a memento
like this? How would who? – like this, near the German
frontier ... The answer: to be the only
claimant in a wood without existence
is a clinched mistake, bitter, the question is void.

Condamn'd

On pure tablecloth, amid cutlery
and lesser glimmering useful pots and cellars,
stood a five-inch-high silverplate dodo,
recent gift to our host. Leaning forward somewhat
on large strong silver feet, claws well spread. I said,
very topically, that is exactly the stance

one needs on this ice, weight forward. Then a lively
disagreement took flight around the bird. Was it
sailors off colonizing ships who fanned out
scooping them up, sitting ducks with meaty
bodies, thighs? Or was it, as the other au-fait
camp maintained, ships' dogs that slavering went

hoovering up the dodo eggs from that clumpy
defenceless paradise. Or else, I conjectured,
looking closer, weight forward, at features scored
darker-true with robust craft, they just got too damn
ugly, and male (silver) dodos, weight backwards, couldn't
bring themselves to do the necessary any more.

Traversal

Get through the day, traverse the day, and you
will be taken by the loop of night, like a swimmer
rotating, tucked, at the end of a racing length

and rammed out, prodded, into the level next.
Rolled up in a pledged circularity of lengths
of day, laid out however all in the same

direction, called time. The 'lengths' also 'no-lengths'
since time has more than once been rumbled, as trumped up ...
When you do turn really old, circle-winding your red

clockwork torch in the brief pew shared with long haul
kindly wife at the bring-your-own-candle candlelit
carol service, and it whirrs, buzzes egregiously,

you don't care a sod, you wind it when you have to.
Or you're a ninety-year-old famous lady author
of children's books, and after the Literary

Festival Tent interview your interviewer
kisses you gallantly on both cheeks. One kiss lands right
on your mini cheek-mike, with a loud plosion which

kisses everyone in the audience's ear. You go
home and contend (just as you did in your prime)
that each day is as full as a page but the

24-hour interval, between each bedtime
mirror face towelling and the last, is moot, fine as
a page edge, in fact reads as non-existent.

Timeless Fernlike Party Horns

shrilled out unfurling (then drooped
then out again) but the three Ninja
Turtle boys united in blurting
'This party's crap!', there were cross words
finally with the departing hired
fairy and then it only for
the single mother remained
to watch the orange juice dry
(on furnished brown tableglint).

Deal with It

Our hostess stayed behind to deal
with the slug infestation. Catching up
in the stove-warm mountain hut, she
served us imitations of a salted slug's
shrinking-back scream ... In lowland silence
it fell to me one time, taking care
of a dead ewe which had gravitated to
the lowest end setting. Tilting and pouring

from belly into meagre stream a thick stream
of maggots, I lightened my load. Before
wrenching incoherent carcass from weed-rich
brook. Still lighter the load if you shift
a dead ewe under its own power. A ghostly
ear twitch. Narrow inspection made
the sheep painfully get up: I drove it slowly
across the whole grey field to a better

place to stink. Stale crimson sheet of wound
caked down one side. As it went – living dead –
it stumbled twice, haggard (Lazarus
on Calvary) under my hard man eyes.
Unlike the girl's at a bullfight, on youth
travels together. Who was fine with
the spectacle, and picador poles' streaked
waggle, but in the moment the bull got

perforated between the shoulders, on and
in, a crumpling tearburst beside me.
So explosive as to carry almost a smell.
She lacked the small cavern of cruelty you

and I can locate inside us if needed,
and breathe through. The impassiveness at least.
She was as bad as that rat-eyed (cartoon)
relisher in movie-house rows of distraught.

The Tuft, the Pierced Throne and the English Duke

Louis Quatorze, the radio
reminded us, was
married to Marie Treize.
May well have bestowed
l'amour l'aprés-midi,
one up in the gilded dim.
Certainly he was drawn
to the *toison de trois heures*
on his mistresses
of languid good name.
When, that is, he was done
with the call of his *chaise
percée,* where he would be
assisted with chamberly
discretion. Of which
in England *His Grace,*
so Aubrey heard, showed
scant, during a Geometries
-reading just for him
but sat *at mastrupation,*
attention level
commensurately low.

Sacred Shell

The most powerful thing on two pages:
a poem. And yet I might go along with
the many at rock festivals who shake that
Make Poetry History wristband (at a rough
glance). Now Poetry's own festivals –

a playroom-yellow converted chapel
or meeting house, an exception reading
gangly, discerning, rising to
his pocket public. For all his power
a toy world. Which the real public

don't mind in its capsules, why should they,
they're across the ancient street in pubs
and stony attitudes watching England
quietly lose the World Cup quarter-finals.
And, quiet or no, they don't hear what's intoned

in the word-weighing chapel thirty yards off,
toy-high ... Kindly somebody stooped to
give me a glossy slim mag they'd put by,
in pleasing font a solitary *Poetry*
on the front. Of interest darling? Um

no: a fashion (art swirl) supplement
flattering its wares in a way – duh-*uh* – no-one's
about to misunderstand. Asset-stripping,
and why not, an empty shell. Empty but
for the nacreous within, reading themselves.

Facebook

He said he was joining Facebook because
not joining has become such a statement,
he didn't want to stand out. I said
I know, it was like, *not* going up at the
end of the sentence is a real statement too.

Shove Ten

Phone boxes everywhere empty now
(except in Soho where occasional
figures pick up, unconvincingly
chat into a void as they memorize

numbers still palimpsesting the walls).
Think back to the impatience outside,
fug on entry, concrete floor, the urban
tomb smell of tobacco and the black

receiver smell worst, livingly
unpleasant without fail, it will
be no pleasanter after you've put in
your 10pennyworth ... Everywhere now

mobiles, lightweight and less smell share.
Keep pressing the small handset button
with your nail to turn it off (like
strangling on till the victim goes limp).

The Residue

An erudite woman, friend of mine, hot from
dumpling banquets in her honour in China
and chaser of tortoise, confirmed we eat fairly
much exclusively herbivores. Carnivores
turn us off. Then it occurred: on tost

rafts or come the apocalypse we would swerve
our attention first on vegetarians,
only natural. In general, a voice added,
our flesh is supposed to be like
pork. The woman (the friend) young in the face,

nourished by marriage, by chance herself
vegetarian, had between knife and fork
her plot. Dinner surged with the jokes,
*All-Vegetarian Menu, Veg
and 2 Veg,* placards huffing outside

Save Our Bacon ... The washing-up mine.
I went to clean, sponge the table and –
jokers departed – sent skimming a pair
of stylish, geneticist's specs with
an arm snapped, hers (and I twigged. Piggy).

County Town Pre-Christmas

Pavarotti is dead, Popeye's Bluto.
Short grass stems poke sparsely through the
unusual snow like accurate dark green
stubble on a Ron Mueck hugeness head.

In the air a hint of angels with waxed legs
(not those little haired casual sitting
crossed on a wall ones). Cold dusking blue
in the main square, elongated.

Rising, falling of glossy worn cream horses.
Carousel music broad frisky and eery.
Some decades back, 'chainsaw crucifix'
contests in the town. How long a bloke could

hold two chainsaws out level, till tremble
goes shake. It might become *no* crucifix
if only Christ could find the backbone
to worm saw round, and snarl through rood.

Bump and Slash

Outside someone was making those inverted comma
fingerhooks, to show the night was only a citation.
A mayfly, to name names, holding up its vivid-brown,
seaweed-brown candelabra, its punctuation antlers,
and bumping the glass like a big boy to get in, its goal
to join the illuminations. But imperviously denied
by me three feet away, sitting over a text deleting
commas like a referee allowing a football game to flow.

Cameraderie

They suddenly bobble, the silhouetted
two heads in the car in front – even as
you're finding it funny, your head
bobbles too (dip in the road). And sometimes

a roadworks sign seeking to harness
sweet reason: speed restrictions in Austria
soft sold with a LIMIT AUS FAIRNESS.
Disarming the touring Anglophone.

But then universal and focused
is the courtesy of drivers, *when few.*
Friends crossing Norway, what with smokes
frowned on nowadays, resting their two-car

convoy halfway under some dulled
pines, offer CDs tapped from the pouch.
Drivers in the night all over the world
dip graciously, or might just – flashback – die.

We All Call Her That

Granny said 'The lack of a crossword
knocks the stuffing out of Sundays.'

My other half said 'I find my deodorant
failing at Granny's' (the superwarmth

much topped up by white swivel heater).
I said 'Sitting on chocolate is good

for your teeth, Granny' (she'd sat some into
her sofa and had to 'mop it up' but

not by swallowing on this occasion).
And child said – fair point – 'Old people

don't play with old people' (scotching
my someone-for-everyone visit plans).

'I come back all blotchy with widened pores,'
pursued the deodorant-mentioner.

'Peking used to be famous,' said Granny
petulantly, 'but not ... not ...' *'Beijing?'*

we offered and, helpful, 'Same with Bombay.
Bombay used to be famous. But ... *Mumbai* ...'

Animation in old people's faces,
I said (to myself once, detained

by my father's last passport-booth photo),
is often founded on fright and confusion.

Shotput

Broaching German airspace, gazing down, thumb at chin,
fingers to forehead, the phrase is 'Aryan calipers'.
Feuchte Aussprache is when the wet morsels of your speech
go to join, like a tributary, the mountain torrent
you lederhose stiffly beside, or smatter the upturned

rumpus round your Munich soapbox in a seminal year.
Who is it who's like a third of the triple portrait
of Charles I by Van Dyck, same tendresse for authority
and chink-of-weakness face? An eternal temptation, to pop
from a privileged position in the tiered-up rear entourage

an apple or (shotput) shot into the palm of that wristback salute.
Whose origin was, the wish to lie back homoerotically
with the thousand-quill forward-leaning Heils, not clash,
be different, totalitarianly individual
and be sexy. The origin of the thousand-

goose-steps-arrayed? Small boots. The repeated need to smash
the inner heel down and back, reaping toe-space. Airspace, German,
and the concern, gazing down, that barely 21st
century true blondes are being painted into a corner
by globalization. And then maybe painted out of it.

Leaf Couplet

I discovered in the chained
library of my mind,
between two pages, on a time-grubbed
vellum remnant an unsigned
medieval frag., last couplet:

Wel I lye inne bedde lyk a sak.
If I ly liche a leef, I am syk.

Done Good

Society blent in its updived city
and divorcity. Those once 'within earshot'
have network or not. We have John Cusack
too, not so much typecast as typecoated in
his rational wintercoat of dark wool. There was
a tendency, recorded by the unstinting

Boswell, to launch every polite combative
remark, riposte, with *Sir*. 'Sir, these are not …', 'Sir, you
will allow …', 'Sir, I confess …'. A habit in some
quarters gracefully returning with *Dude*. 'Dude,
you wish,' 'Dude, wassup?', 'Dude, no way'. And great
finickitiness there used to be also – as

when, earlier still, Sir Thomas Browne chafed
at the glib and senseless depiction in art
of Adam and Eve with navels. The very
first of us, with navels? Navels back to Whom?
But we are not so fussed, and have at a number
of sites umbilical stem cells on the go nicely.

The Taxi Stand, South Wales

In his innocence he refused to give
the big man a potato chip.
The rude man uttered again
'Give us a chip'. The small plump man,
blank face and innocence, didn't.
Sitting unfocused on the cab rank bench
late at night in his white shirt, chopped lank
hair, he had every right to refuse.
Even the large man's nettled fists.
The girl (my source) was pressed between.
The chip fancier – with ominous retro
brylcreem cliff – tore past her sober
body at him, all three strangers.
Then, face blank or indignant,
the dumpy man had an epileptic fit.
The rough man backed off. A lady scurried
at last from her cabin to help the distressed,
whom she remembered. 'Sorry, mate, sorry.
If I'd known there was something wrong with you …', went
the big bloke and rode out his cab in due course,
limbering up with threats for household.
The small man, for being unwise,
had shed both front teeth and would do again.
Fantastically unwise.

Guest on Guest

Soon the great apes will all be eaten
by forest miners and others. Time is wind

to the meteorologist, and the future
a scrutable whorl. A figure-of-eight

head movement, on a railway platform
of the subcontinent, blends agreement,

caveats and transcendence (not just yes
to a cup of tea) ... It cloudily warm

enough to sit out, across a slick
West London pavement table, a friend with

fresh straggly beard said 'letting nature take
its course'. I leant in, deducted his specs.

The table elsewhere under which, as guest
couple, my socked foot latched on her bare one

'like a flipper', she harked back with makings
of repugnance. Give me the woman sign – waist

and hips – alone, dazzling in the animal
kingdom. Because – baby brain size? Or

from such long lying close, in the scrub,
with man's heavy arm of unusual

affection draped round, wearing no mean groove.

Train of Empties

Some teenage Germans, between
the wars, studied for the Abitur,
some for the abattoir. To this day
Groucho's eyebrows, when they bounce up

in black volleys from his clenched cigar,
are shooting high with Jewdar, the suspicion
there's a strolling jew beneath the square-jawed
Californian entrepreneur coming over.

Bandy-legged Gaucho Marx. Not the first
Lion of Jewdar ... Jotted on the spine
of a video cassette in a pile of poor light
was *Docum*(entary): *Antichrist.*

Worm nearer through the niggardly light
and tighten, it's Docum: *Auschwitz.*
Two strands walk innocent, 'Young Bob Dylan
on trolley harmonica' (undersized

freckled aquiline supermarket
boy employee with big hair pushing
bendy hobo train in the carpark rain)
and Laura Like, a new wave German band.

The Cladding

My girlfriend's become my wife and now
takes Full Curve Jeans. When I clamber
into bed on a cold night often
edge closer and closer to
her sleeping body in sinuous
parallel (of foetalists grown up)
till inches away all the way along

I can partake (on the sly) of
the pleasant offshore blast of her heat.
Cladding of heat, draw up to it. In her
territorial waters get moored.
A warm shore-denoting
quillage pencilled (in geography
class) between us, nothing else.

Only magnetically repelling
respect for her sleep keeps us untouching.
Like two hedges of a winding lane
aerially seen as good as touching.
But the thing is, if I maintain
position, I may reputedly snore.
But definitely call on women

to stand up and snore for themselves ...
Before all which, *What's that?* I'd lobbed in
from bedroom to bathroom, at evening's
end. *What?* The sound of unzipping,
sounds promising. It's me unzipping
my tampax bag. What, nothing could
be less promising than that.

Denounce

When even your photo face stops working.
The jaw-rehearsed direct-with-hint-of
face that's seen you through thirty years,
a thousand snaps (cocky in the curtained
booth, unquailing in the sofa group),
starts failing of its magic. You're just as
gross and high-coloured as captured mid-fuss
by your wife's device or someone.
(Only your mirror face with its saving
mobility stands by you.) It dawns on
you, sinking in, that 'I think I look like
this, I think I look like that *but I look
like the fucking other.*' You tell the brother-
in-law in the pub – an aside of toneless
ill-comprehended force, as the holiday
pics skim through lively, smartphone and beer mats –
'I don't know that person, and I don't want to
know them. *Don't know anybody like that.*'

Core Clubs

There was the Hellfire Club
and the sombre choosy rakish
Suicide Club, whose motto was
avant de mourir, mourir.

Teamwork

Bogart, she said, always talks
like he's wearing huge braces.
Oh, wearing both kinds of braces then.
Awful, she said, if there's an intruder
in the house somewhere, and he farts,
you overhear it. Oh, a bummer.
A double unwished whammy.
The garagiste, the MOT man,
said with filthy hands
he wanted to come back as a vicar.
Oh, be careful, you might come back
as the vicarage not the vicar.
And, said a check-out girl, each till's
bleep pitch can be selected.
So you don't think another
till is you. Oh, like in a loud
dance club you mean, when you don't know
who's talking here, who said that last
thing, you or her, ear and mouth.
Let me mention: Stalin was sometimes
called by himself or others Great Leader
And Gardener Of The People.
She said Oh, *and using*
ROUND-UP a bit too freely.

Wales

Savour a beautiful unspoilt landscape
too long and God, embarrassed
by the perfection of his work,
clears his throat, with the sound
of a jet entering the picture.

The Grater

Babies sleep far-sightedly in the
dark, and gulls' eggs have those bloated specks
first rain puts on green weatherproof. In Essex
-Suffolk country, a highly English sign: 'Truly Free

Range Eggs'. To study from the side the whole
limpid thick lens front of a baby's eye behind
which – and not before – they exist, is to take, mind,
nothing from their humanity. When old,

if now they sleep in proper dark, then they'll
see the better. Two changes will come about,
to hatch the end: body disenchantment; and float
the currency of your identity. Half way

along this journey your hand is led across,
in washing a cheese grater up, the soft little
poke-through blisters of your other. Exotic grill
vouchsafings. First run-in with self-tenderness?

A Size or More Down

Damien didn't miss a trick
until he called his 2007
jewelled skull (astute,
not his size) 'For the love of God'.
He didn't fail to mention
or let it be sleuthed, the diamonds
smoothly densely evenly
bedded were in themselves worth
£12m. He failed to mouthe it
'O Death, where is thy bling?'

A Sprinkling

On almost every hill town church door
the rather offensive notices nailing
us tourists: printed shapes of man and woman
side by side, bare-shouldered in singlet,
camisole, her mini-skirt, his shorts and

moustache. Both parties therefore crossed out
with red slashes: banned from entering. Of course
we all quietly entered, semi-clothed, shouldering
door and doorsign open with the minimum
of umbrage. Somewhat offensive nonetheless

except for the banning of moustaches. But when
it came to Dubrovnik, the tourist viscosity
channelling everywhere beneath uncorrupted stone,
tour leaders' squeamish pennants above the ongoing
throng, cameras and mobiles held up on arms or stalks

for any resulting world-famous catch, churches
respectfully negotiated *via the flip-out
camcorder screen,* from entry to exit, I switched
camps. And meditated how personally
to throw out of the temple of Dubrovnik

the changers of 'money into light' (as filming
has been summed up). Soothed by a travel sequence
of loo brushes, though, in each monopolized
or shared toilet, the sphere brush, cube brush, cylinder
brush, ring brush, each of which by a varying

stem I replaced in its customized hole.
When it came to departure, in tiny
Byrnik Airport's Gents, my toes were sprinkled
suddenly in their Birkenstocks, not
disagreeably or irreligiously,

by other gents on the wing flicking
their sink-wet fingers dry, a further plus.
From the shortish queue for the apple-
tolerant bagscan, I got to consider
two or three pairs of young lovers (not yet

as established, stocky, as us church door bods)
involved in their devout parting package:
all-out delivery of the kiss, then
walking away fast without looking back,
suffused with momentous first digestings

and the daze of not wishing to spoil it. In view
from the roll-out steps was the rose-pink mountain
calling, unairportlike, and once inside
the plane, of the 18 people seated nearest
9 needed dark glasses for the eyes in their hair.

Warszawa-Paris

Company well provided
for the lady presumed to be Polish.
Two chubby girls in emphatic spirits
pulling out of Berlin and a young (sole
eye-catching girl on the train) fellow Pole.
She noted them blearily,
stowed by a window, vague on her luck.
The chubby girls snatched their bags at Potsdam

(so lively they'd mixed their trains), the stunner
rustled up predators on the empty seats, left them
for a compartment of shared laughter and ...
burnt predators decamped. The lady remained,
hair the colour-tone of the upholstery,
didn't complain, not spoken before, not about
to now, proved no draw for souls dragging late
luggage and made no attempt to claw back

by relocation her former good thing.
She closed as often as opened her eyes. On closing
the compartment discounted. Some night hours more
along the old German lifeline (Berlin to West)
and – respectable, drained, reading-glasses askew –
she'd dealt herself out across the seats, in general
a similar colour, stockinged feet no
smell, wasn't the problem, door lurch exposing and
unmolested, classed with the compartment lights on.

From the Stack, at a Slant

It is an old image, that from the air
skyscrapers look like gravestones, especially
the elegant flattish ones, downtown
Seattle for instance, a sheaf of gravestones.
It is an old story, that thick boulders
seal places off, caves and tombs. Round here

they also serve to seal off seldom used lay-bys
on leafy roads outside villages,
biblically enough. The intention
not clear, it must be to keep gypsies and
travellers out. In which case the boulders
win no haloes. Those golden outrays

sanctity makes. Being the tails at a guess
of arrows of gold lodged in the head. All along
the central barrier of the London
Westway flyover, the streetlamps had gone
dark, lopped off low, the stumps assuaged in tatty
lemon night-vis plastic-sacking bandages.

Separate Sightings

One gleaming white motor home I spotted
was towing on a fixed-bar a Smart car:
swish yacht and dinghy.
Another white motor home
I spotted, wilderness-headed,
had a wheelchair strapped on behind,
cleaving to it in a black sheath but partly
showing through, tragic spokes and gleaming.

Planted in the Back of Our Minds

Abruptly with warning everyone in their scuffed
armchairs sat forward. The BBC had chosen
to release across the country east to west
a batch of news spores really damaging

which for some years and reason they'd kept wrapped:
almost all Britain's ash trees would get 'dieback'
and perish. Timeline: 20 years. Dendrologists,
newspapers, nursery-owners, were on message

in this. Viewers leant forward into a bitter
spore-laden easterly of blackleaf prediction.
But as quickly the wind fell, the media after
a week dropped the story. Had it been said in fact?

What could a body do? Were thick-limbed favourites
already collapsing in gloom outline across
the window? Teacups of other news to the fore?
We sat back somnolent (and awaited dieback).

Handover by Night

The Queen has passed the dream baton on.
It's no longer the Queen offering one
tea on a tartan rug, herself strangely supple,
knees to the side. Or the Queen, her handbag
laid faintly gruff beside her, on the passenger
seat of the camper van, burrowing into France.
I suppose she's not the archetype she was.
It's Putin one now hangs out with
in a Bucharest café, with talk of
going on to a club he knows.
And in this role, and pale windcheater,
he's surprisingly – affable, gets almost
personal, almost raises his eyes –
good value and unthreatening, I have found.

Attached Cabin

In a small shining cabin
beneath the vast negligible.
The self

often at a loss to locate
a shoe horn, hence the shoe horn
of the index finger.

As for any snoring, it
exists only in a parallel
universe of grotesque accusations.

True that I was extra-
terrestrial at our dinner party,
sober, drug-free and swingeingly

out of my skull, but able
to put the sufficing words in place
with mile-long puppet sticks or tongs.

After dense follow-up kitchen
duties, I sat down on the sofa with
an exhaustion so deep as to bring

the dizzy rotation underwater
squiggle I used to enjoy
falling forwards into a swimming

pool, head to breast, handclasp behind.
As my weight hit the sofa a backcurl
in the black, of watery stars. Human:

dogs that lick us, mobiles accept
our code. To the tune and tempo
of *Security* – sung out by Etta

James or Otis Redding – my own song
Obscurity, which goes down very
well too, loam succour, warm-fail.

Cloud Measure

How big a cloud, really? Tricky
to tell. Unless ... by the shadow.
A 3-field cloud. The sunboat puts out
at last to blue, from a refulgent
cloudcoast. Thank you for the many

lit walks, as it were trips by
sunboat, jointly. And back, into the
cloudhouse. Admittedly, without
any clouds, by which shall be meant
apart ones with blue between, is lonely.

All blue is. Or all cloud (or no wind).
All blue sky in a painting
or photograph is kind of crass.
But on a field it does set the kiss of
light that says you need never grow up.

And if, on holiday, you find
yourselves with car, there's a gambit:
you can spurt down the coast
out of the (province-sized) gathering fist
of cloud like a bar of soap.

Woven Alike

The faery ring fortification she raised, from
the floor, was woven of soft toys and hard toys
alike (floppy dragons and headbutt babies)
for walls of good tensility, green-and-red
heightfastness and craggy storm resistance.
A trip to the zoo was imminent to see
'… mountain gorillas and stick insects,' she said

concluding the list. Also, that when she'll be
queen, she'll have her telephone brought to her
(on a cushion?) and play Candy Crush Saga
the whole day. I told her, not unpleasingly,
'You have biscuits in trees and pearls between your toes.'
(She'd left some biscuits behind in a tree
fork, they were wettened through by rain. And what

extruded at bed-time from between her toes
wasn't gunge after all but pearls or similar
which had come unstuck from her tiara.) She
told me straight, in a delayed but studied
return compliment, positioned to judge,
that my legs were very hairy, my head
like a drum and I myself like a vampire.

Surrender Hanky

Mankind's been dealt a different hand:
we have an opposing tomb.
  * * *
I shudder therefore I think.
Obit. So be it. Sob it.
  * * *
Why's a monkey called a monkey?
It is a human *manqué*.

In the Lieu

One of those enormous 'spiders with
long bodies sitting behind the vitamins,'
she alerted me. My small computer

no sooner opened than alerted me
Your Companion is at Risk. Turning
my face grave. But, on blinking and checking:

the soothsayer rather, that was at risk
according to McAfee each (harassing
solicitous pop-up) time. My companion's

chief threat remained Louisa, whose 'sports bra
gives her the edge' in their weekly tennis.
Although, when her own 1kg yellow

handweights arrived, 'They'll send my bingo
wings packing,' she claimed. And when she
laid a slender (false) further claim to

big forearms, I acquiesced and warmly
averred, but not that wittingly, 'Yes, we
were drawn to each other by our big forearms.'

She was able to characterize the skin
near my eye as 'a starburst', by indoor
daylight, appraising around in

the lieu of crow's feet. *A happy couple is a lonely couple,* one might enlarge in the Russian Paradox tradition.

Thought Through

In a village a sign outside a house
directed at occasional through-traffic
read 'Oven Ready Poultry'. What did it mean?
That freshly plucked chickens were now for sale,
and if no takers would be frozen by nightfall?
Or that backyard chickens pecking about
could be knocked off there and then, were ready
to be killed, were mentally 'oven ready'?

Ledges

The search for life in The Universe:
the search of course for no life, no threat
to our triste colossal significance.
Nobody out there to observe
'Full earth tonight', a brilliant help.

Brancusi's Beginning Of The World:
a lot like his Sculpture For The Blind.
Great marble eggs coning longer one end
– as do the Guillemot's which, the NatHist
side-gallery apprises us late in the day,

are designed to roll only in tight
limited circles, on cliff ledges and
yet safe. For the blackness of the world
is no weeping matter (hardbitten
stock riposte), but at least in Finnish

midwinter bars you can pull up a stool
and order a pint of light, pineal pint.
Bright as the Albert St council estate
so crusted with walkway lights it can
be clocked from space like Belgium. The Mars probe

has sent us a photo of the vast Mons
Olympus crater: slender black ring
on grey, very like a (News) IVF
microscope egg, awaiting the
momentarily distorting needle push.

Whichever

One for the mood.
Two can condescend.
'Circle as many
as are true' – this is
a family motto,
ancient. *Or* kicks off
a multiple choice exam.
Other mottos (choose
and loop). 'I eschew the cud
of small talk' (from the Latin).
Or 'It is good to
go to bed with a light heart,
empty arse.' 'If something hurts,
bite it'. More now, *'The perks
of non-stardom are infinite.'*

Tourists at the End

She stepped from the car to course water through
the grape bunch we took to the beach, it plumping
its transparent plastic bag like a brain.
The permanent double lines down the middle
of these dry sinuous coast roads cry wolf.

Soon the cry in the car, regarding family
drink bottle, went up, 'No salami backwash!'
(targeting me) ... If we shut the night-hot room's
window we heard the air-conditioning,
lumped on the wall, take the part of the sea. All night

underpants, not all day – kind of a reversal.
And tourists, as the season tapers, are flushed
– depopulating roads, vistas, rooms – first
from the cape, the tip, of a Peloponnese
finger, like stragglers from a museum's

far end, ten minutes before closing time (by
persistent attendant-shepherds) ... The sea
demonstrates, by turning out tumbling floral
swimtrunks' sunlit white net pockets in shingly surf
again, a bather's ultimate poverty.

www.ingramcontent.com/pod-product-compliance
Lightning Source LLC
Chambersburg PA
CBHW021128080526
44587CB00012B/1192